Buckinghamshire's Lost Railwa

by
Keith Scholey

Cheddington Station, which is still open. The branch
line to Aylesbury curves away to the right.

Text © Keith Scholey, 2004.
First published in the United Kingdom, 2004,
by Stenlake Publishing
Telephone: 01290 551122
Printed by Cordfall Ltd, Glasgow, G21 2QA

ISBN 1 84033 275 1

The publishers regret that they cannot supply
copies of any pictures featured in this book.

PICTURE ACKNOWLEDGEMENTS
The publishers wish to thank the following for contributing photographs
to this book: John Alsop for the front cover, pages 1, 13, 15, 19, 24, 27–29,
35, 43, 45, the inside back cover, and the back cover; Richard Casserley for
pages 2–12, 14, 16–18, 20–23, 25, 26, 30–34, 36–40, 42, 44 and 47; and the
author for pages 41, 46 and 48.

Ivatt 2-6-2 tank No. 41275 at Aylesbury High Street Station, 1 March 1952.

INTRODUCTION

Buckinghamshire's first railways were built in the mid-1830s. The London & Birmingham Railway (part of the London & North Western Railway from 1846 and now the southern section of the West Coast main line) cut across the north-east corner of the county. The Great Western Railway (out of Paddington), on the other hand, ran neatly through the southernmost tip. These were important main lines, but were essentially peripheral to the county. In between was a vast expanse of agricultural land dotted with tiny hamlets and small market towns. The history of railway development in Buckinghamshire is the penetration of this 'heart of darkness' by the shining light of Victorian progress in the shape of the steam locomotive.

The first invasions into this heartland were made in the early 1850s. In the north the Buckinghamshire Railway, a London & North Western affiliate, sent out tendrils from Bletchley to Oxford, with a branch to Banbury. In the south the Wycombe Railway, sponsored by the Great Western, connected the prosperous market town of High Wycombe to the Great Western main line at Maidenhead. A decade later the centre of the county was covered by extensions of the Wycombe Railway to Oxford via Thame and Aylesbury. In the late 1860s the Aylesbury & Buckingham Railway formed a link between the Great Western and London & North Western systems, and the early 1870s saw the branch network completed with lines to Watlington, Marlow and Brill.

At this stage things might well have rested. However, a prosperous regional company, the Manchester, Sheffield & Lincolnshire Railway, was looking for an entry into London. To assist it the Metropolitan Railway, the original London Underground, built towards the north, reaching Aylesbury in 1892 and afterwards taking over the old Aylesbury & Buckingham Railway with the rather unwelcome gift of the very unprofitable Brill Branch thrown in.

The Great Central (as the Manchester, Sheffield & Lincolnshire became) reached a junction with the Met at Quainton Road in 1898. Due to corporate wranglings, as well as severe curvature on the Met line (which was to result in a terrible accident at Aylesbury on 23 December 1904), the situation was still unsatisfactory. The Great Central teamed up with the Great Western, which wanted to shorten its route to Birmingham, to form the Great Western & Great Central Joint Railway. Running from Northolt in Middlesex to Ashendon Junction, this utilised the central section of the old Wycombe Railway. The entire scheme was complete by 1910, by which time the Met and the Great Central had come to an agreement to form a joint committee to run the line from Harrow to Quainton Road, as well as what had become the Verney Junction and Brill branches. The Great

Western & Great Central retained a purpose as part of the Great Western's Birmingham line.

The compulsory reorganisation of the railways in 1923 allocated the London & North Western to the London, Midland & Scottish Railway (LMS), while the Great Central was merged into the London & North Eastern Railway (LNER). The Great Western remained unchanged within the county. Such developments did not affect service patterns, but the formation of London Transport in 1933 had a more dramatic impact: the Met lost its independence and within a few years the Brill and Verney Junction lines were axed.

Nationalisation in 1948 at first had little effect. The old London & North Western Aylesbury Branch was closed in 1953, but this had been on the cards for years. The 1960s, as elsewhere, was a period of decimation for the railways and within a decade the branch lines had virtually disappeared. The only survivors were the ex-Great Western Aylesbury Branch, the Bletchley–Bedford line, the tiny Marlow Branch and the Chesham Branch. In addition, the old Great Central main line was shut down. While this was probably justifiable at the time, railway privatisation and the present rapid increase in rail use could have given this line a new lease of life. Today, services in the county are almost entirely of the through main line or outer suburban pattern.

Calvert Station, facing south, 25 March 1961. This was a typical station of the Great Central's London extension.

Aylesbury Branch (Cheddington to Aylesbury) *

		Stations closed	Date
Passenger service withdrawn	2 February 1953	Aylesbury (first)	16 June 1889
Distance	6.9 miles	Aylesbury (second) **	2 February 1953
Company	London & North Western		

Aylesbury Station, 19 March 1949. The overall roof arrangement was widely used by the LNWR for its branch line termini.

* The closed station on this line that was in Hertfordshire was Marston Gate.

** This replaced Aylesbury (first) and was renamed Aylesbury High Street on 25 September 1950.

Aylesbury High Street, 24 January 1953.

Although two miles of the middle stretch of this branch lay in Hertfordshire, both ends were in Buckinghamshire. Promoted and built by the Aylesbury Railway – a locally organised company firmly under the thumb of the London & Birmingham Railway – the line was ceremonially opened on 10 June 1839. Although it was built as the first section of a projected line to Oxford, all its life it remained a simple country branch line from the Euston–Birmingham main line to the county town. The local company was absorbed into the London & North Western Railway in 1846. The branch ran straight and level across the Vale of Aylesbury. Its primary business was in agricultural produce, especially milk from local dairy farming. General supplies to Aylesbury and coal, both domestic and for the gasworks, were also transported. Additionally, the line transported the products of Aylesbury's various industries: printing (including the famous *Readers Digest*), brewing and basket weaving. Apart from the very earliest years, the branch never saw intensive use and was closed for passengers on 2 February 1953 (remaining open for goods until 2 December 1963). Much of the route has since been reabsorbed into the farmland through which it was built.

Banbury Branch (Verney Junction to Banbury Merton Street) *

		Stations closed	Date
Passenger service withdrawn	Buckingham to Banbury: 31 December 1960; Verney Junction to Buckingham: 7 September 1964.	Padbury	7 September 1964
		Buckingham	7 September 1964
Distance	21.4 miles	Radclive Halt	31 December 1960
Company	London & North Western	Water Stratford Halt	31 December 1960
		Fulwell & Westbury	31 December 1960

Padbury Station, looking towards Verney Junction, 30 April 1960.

* Closed stations on this line that were in Northamptonshire were Brackley and Farthinghoe. The closed station in Oxfordshire was Banbury Merton Street.

Buckingham Station, looking towards Banbury, 15 February 1956.

This line, about seven miles of which lies in Buckinghamshire, started life as the Buckingham & Brackley Junction Railway which was authorised in 1846. This railway was the northern arm of a landowners' scheme to develop the area (see Oxford Branch). Initially, the terminus was to have been Brackley, but the following year powers were obtained to extend to Banbury and the company was consolidated with the future Oxford Branch as the Buckinghamshire Railway. For strategic reasons the extension to Banbury was pushed by the London & North Western, which had gained financial control over the local enterprise (and was later to merge with it), as it hoped to poach the Birmingham & Oxford Railway from the Great Western and in doing so defend its monopoly trade with England's second city. However, although the Banbury Branch was laid out with room for double track, this development did not come to pass and the line always remained a single-track rural branch line. The line was opened on 1 May 1850 for passengers and two weeks later for goods.

Radclive Halt, looking towards Verney Junction, 30 April 1960. This was opened on 13 August 1956.

Passenger traffic was always relatively light and was chiefly made up of villagers going to market. In Victorian times the line was a viable option for London-bound passengers from Banbury; however, the completion in 1910 of the Great Western's Birmingham line stole most of this trade. Buckingham was still important, for this was the station for Stowe, which was first a palatial residence and later a famous private school. To boost falling usage, diesel railcars started using the branch in 1956 and new halts were opened at Radclive and Water Stratford. The experiment seems to have been a failure and although trains were often packed at peak hours, off-peak trains ran empty. Rising fares and the physical deterioration of stations discouraged travel, while rising wages drove revenues well into the red. The line was closed in two stages, the final train to Banbury departing on the last day of 1960 while the Verney to Buckingham section lingered on for a few more years.

Fulwell & Westbury Station, looking towards Verney Junction, 14 March 1955. This station was opened as Westbury Crossing on 1 August 1879. It was renamed on 1 October 1880.

Goods traffic was concentrated on the thriving south Midlands town of Banbury. However, milk, especially from the local country stations, was also transported to a factory opposite Buckingham Station. Cattle were also carried for the local agricultural market. The line north of Buckingham was closed for goods in 1964, the southern section following three years later. The old route can be traced although parts have been absorbed into surrounding farmland.

Brill Branch (Quainton Road to Brill)

Passenger service withdrawn	30 November 1935	*Stations closed*	*Date*
Distance	6.3 miles	Westcott	30 November 1935
Company	Metropolitan & Great Central Joint Committee	Wotton	30 November 1935
		Wood Siding	30 November 1935
Stations closed	*Date*	Brill	30 November 1935
Waddesdon Road	30 November 1935		

Waddesdon Road Station, looking towards the level crossing with the goods siding on the left, 8 April 1933. The station was known as Waddesdon until 1 October 1922.

Waddesdon Road, 8 April 1933. Built in 1866, locomotive No. 23 worked on the Brill Branch from around 1915 until 1933 and is now preserved at London's Transport Museum.

The Brill Branch had its origins in the Wotton Tramway, which was built for the Duke of Buckingham to serve his estate and ran almost entirely on his own land. The first section of the tramway, from Quainton Road on the Aylesbury & Buckingham Railway to near the Duke's residence at Wotton, was opened in March 1871, with completion to a station serving the hilltop village of Brill coming a year later. Initially worked by horses, a primitive single cylinder locomotive was in use by early 1872. This was built by Aveling & Porter and resembled their famous traction engines. Around the same time a passenger service was introduced. Plans were developed for extension to Oxford and in 1894 the line was renamed the Oxford & Aylesbury Tramroad. But despite this work on the project never started.

Westcott Station. Milk was an important commodity for the Brill Branch; note the milk churns on the platform.

The Metropolitan Railway took over working of the line in 1899 (although the local company continued 'on paper' until 1940) and the Brill Branch became the outer limits of Baker Street's far-flung empire. The Met reconditioned the line and began to work it with its own superannuated stock which included two A Class 4-4-0 tank engines and carriages which dated back to the original Underground of the 1860s. After the Met was merged into London Transport in 1933, the new organisation sensibly decided to close the branch and, much loved but little used, it saw its last service two years later.

Wotton Station, *c.*1905.

The branch was lightly built and steeply graded and for part of its route ran adjacent to existing roads. The country it ran through was pretty but entirely rural and dominated by big landed estates. Naturally agriculture was a primary concern, especially the flourishing milk trade. In the 1880s the line was heavily trafficked by building materials for the construction of Baron Rothschild's Waddesdon Manor. On completion a siding was laid in to deliver coal and other supplies to the manor's gasworks at Westcott. Supplies, especially coal, were also delivered to Wotton House via a short branch.

Metropolitan Railway locomotive No. 23 and coach No. 45 at Wood Siding with the 3.07 p.m. from Brill, 22 June 1935.

In late Victorian days a brickworks flourished at Brill. After its closure in 1911 the siding which served it was utilised by a firm manufacturing agricultural machinery, which for a while brought much needed trade to the line. By the early 1930s competition from road transport and other rail lines in the area had virtually stripped the line of goods traffic and this ceased at the time of passenger closure.

'Brill No. 1', a Manning Wardle 0-6-0 saddle tank, at Brill Station *c.*1910.

Metropolitan Railway No. 41 at Brill with the 12.05 p.m. service from Quainton Road, 15 March 1930.

Dunstable Branch (Leighton Buzzard to Dunstable North) *

Passenger service withdrawn 30 June 1962 *Distance* 6.8 miles
Company London & North Western

The route of the 'Dunstable Dasher', this line, which ran from the Euston main line to a station on the outskirts of the old Bedfordshire market town, opened on 1 June 1848. General goods traffic continued for four years after passenger closure, with some traffic on a small section of the route lasting until 1969. Around half a mile of the line, in the immediate vicinity of Leighton Buzzard Station, was in Buckinghamshire.

* Closed stations on this line that were in Bedfordshire were Stanbridgeford and Dunstable North.

Great Central main line (Quainton Road to Rugby Central) *

Passenger service withdrawn	3 September 1966	*Stations closed*	*Date*
Distance	38.6 miles	Calvert	4 March 1963
Company	Great Central		

Calvert Station, looking north, 16 June 1957. The island platform was typical of the stations on this line.

As noted in the introduction, the Great Central Railway (formerly the Manchester, Sheffield & Lincolnshire) built southward from Nottingham in the 1890s. With a view to fast running the London extension was built with only gentle curves and no level crossings. However, contrary to popular belief the new line was not built for passenger traffic (which failed to substantially materialise); freight traffic, especially coal and fish, was always much more important. After the Grouping of 1923, and particularly after Nationalisation, the *raison d'être* of the line disappeared. However, there was still considerable traffic well into the 1950s. Local services were withdrawn in 1963, with the last express a few years later. The line as far as Calvert is still in use for a rubbish disposal plant, but the rest has been abandoned. The eight miles or so in Buckinghamshire traversed a sparsely populated area, yielding revenue only from a large brickworks.

* The closed station on this line that was in Oxfordshire was Finmere. Closed stations in Northamptonshire were Brackley, Helmdon, Culworth, Woodford and Charwelton. The closed station in Warwickshire was Braunston.

Newport Pagnell Branch (Wolverton to Newport Pagnell)

Passenger service withdrawn	5 September 1964	*Stations closed*	*Date*
Distance	4.2 miles	Bradwell	5 September 1964
Company	London & North Western	Great Linford	5 September 1964
		Newport Pagnell	5 September 1964

Bradwell Station, *c.*1911.

Great Linford Station, looking towards Wolverton, 25 July 1959. Note the LMS-style sign board.

Like many other branch lines, this was promoted and built under the auspices of an independent local company. The Newport Pagnell Railway was ostensibly built to link the old market town of Newport Pagnell to the main line near the pleasing red-brick village of Wolverton. However, this local company was backed by the London & North Western which was primarily interested in transporting its employees from the housing estate at New Bradwell to the Wolverton works. From Linford to Newport the line was constructed on an infilled canal, but apart from this oddity there were few notable features. The branch opened to passengers on 2 September 1867, over a year after goods trains had first used the line. An extension to Olney was planned but the project was dropped, although not until after a considerable amount of grading had been carried out and a substantial bridge at Newport constructed.

The end of the line at Newport Pagnell Station, 10 April 1948.

'Newport Nobby', as the little branch train was known, was usually quite full. Partly this was market trade to and from Newport Pagnell and Wolverton, especially from the intermediate villages. However, the main source of income was derived from workers travelling to the extensive railway construction and repair shops at Wolverton and the adjacent McCorquodale's printing works. By the early 1960s passenger traffic on the branch was in decline as short trips of this sort were now usually taken by car or bus. However, another factor in the closure was the impending rundown of Wolverton works.

Class 2P 2-6-2T No. 41222 at Newport Pagnell with the 10.00 a.m. service from Wolverton (with coaches Nos. 17909 and 24483), 12 January 1952.

Goods traffic was mostly of a general nature and was quite considerable – a south curve from Bradwell towards Bletchley was installed in the 1880s exclusively for freight use. As it was elsewhere in the area, milk was the staple of the two village stations. Other commodities handled included lime from the works at Bradwell. The line was closed for goods in 1967. The greater part of the trackbed has been reconditioned for use as a country walk and hikers can have a pleasant picnic at the remains of the two intermediate stations.

Northampton Branch (Oakley Junction to Harding Street Junction) *

Passenger service withdrawn	5 March 1962	*Stations closed*	*Date*
Distance	19.4 miles	Olney	5 March 1962
Company	Midland		

Olney Station, looking towards Northampton, 27 March 1954.

* The closed station on this line that was in Bedfordshire was Turvey. The closed stations in Northamptonshire were Piddington and Northampton St Johns.

Olney Station, 16 October 1962.

The Midland's Northampton Branch was in many ways a typical rural branch line. Characteristically, it was constructed by a small local company, the Bedford & Northampton Railway, which was set up in the heyday of branch line construction in the mid-1860s. The line opened on 10 June 1872, after some delays presumably caused by the usual shortage of capital. It suffered from severe gradients – with several stretches of 1 in 60 and one of 1 in 75 – illustrative of the low standard of construction of many branch lines. Unusually, however, it was originally double track throughout. According to the pattern, after a decade or so the local company was eaten up by the Midland giant (which had always worked the line). As was often the case the line was enthusiastically built in anticipation of extensive prospective traffic which failed to arrive. Just as typically, the branch suffered the same fate as many a branch line and closed in the 1960s. The greater part of the line was closed for goods not long after passenger closure and its route has been largely absorbed back into the surrounding countryside. About seven miles of the line was in Buckinghamshire, the only station on this stretch being Olney, built to serve the large village of the same name.

Oxford Branch (Bletchley to Oxford Rewley Road) *

			Stations closed	Date
Passenger service withdrawn	30 December 1967		Winslow	30 December 1967
Distance	31.5 miles		Verney Junction	30 December 1967
Company	London & North Western		Claydon	30 December 1967
			Marsh Gibbon & Poundon	30 December 1967
Stations closed	*Date*			
Swanbourne	30 December 1967			

Locomotive No. 41275 at Swanbourne Station with the 10.00 a.m. service from Buckingham to Bletchley, 19 April 1959.

* Closed stations on this line that were in Oxfordshire were Launton, Bicester, Wendlebury Halt, Charlton Halt, Doddington Halt, Islip, Oxford Road Halt, Wolvercote Halt, Port Meadow Halt and Oxford.

The rambling country station of Swanbourne, 22 April 1959.

The Oxford Branch was the core of a scheme to develop north Buckinghamshire, planned by a consortium of local landowners headed by the second Duke of Buckingham and Sir Harry Verney. The Buckinghamshire Railway, as it became known, was to consist of a main line from Bletchley to Oxford with branches to Banbury (see Banbury Branch) and Aylesbury (built separately as the Aylesbury & Buckingham Railway). The Buckinghamshire Railway was heavily financed by the London & North Western which was mainly interested in siphoning off some of the lucrative Oxford trade from the Great Western Railway. Construction was relatively easy – the line had few major engineering features – and was opened from Bletchley to Claydon (later Verney) Junction, along with the branch to Banbury via Buckingham, on 1 May 1850, and on to Islip on 1 October 1850. Completion to Oxford took place early the following year. The local company was leased by the London & North Western in 1851 and was absorbed into the same in 1879.

Winslow Station, c.1905. Originally, this station was important as the junction for Banbury, but latterly it was very quiet.

Although around half of the double-track line was in Buckinghamshire, this was not the prosperous half. Passenger traffic was concentrated at the western end, between Bicester and Oxford, since apart from the small town of Winslow, the Buckinghamshire section served only remote villages. The line, however, saw very varied passenger traffic: cross-country services to Cambridge, troop trains to the Central Ordnance Depot at Bicester (from 1940 onwards) and for a short period (1854–61) long distance trains to Worcester and Wolverhampton. The oddest working was possibly the testing of the 'Michelin', a rubber-tyred, petrol-driven rail-bus combo, in 1932. Despite the relatively intensive use of the western section, the line was on the hit list and was closed for passengers at the end of 1967. In 1989 the Bicester to Oxford section was reopened for passengers. Although often proposed, plans to reopen the remainder will probably not come to pass.

Metropolitan Railway locomotive No. 82 at Verney Junction with a Pullman carriage. Built in 1901, No. 82, an E class 0-4-4T, was typical of the engines handling the Met's long-distance trains.

Freight use was also concentrated on the more highly populated western section – especially coal and other goods for Oxford. The Buckinghamshire section was largely agricultural – milk traffic being the staple outbound. There were also large rail-connected brickworks at Claydon and near Bletchley. Under the 1955 railway development plan, the line should have become a major goods link – a concrete bridge over the main lines was built at Bletchley – but these proposals were later dropped. The line was in use until recently for through goods and empty stock transfers. A proposal has been made to reopen at least part of the line.

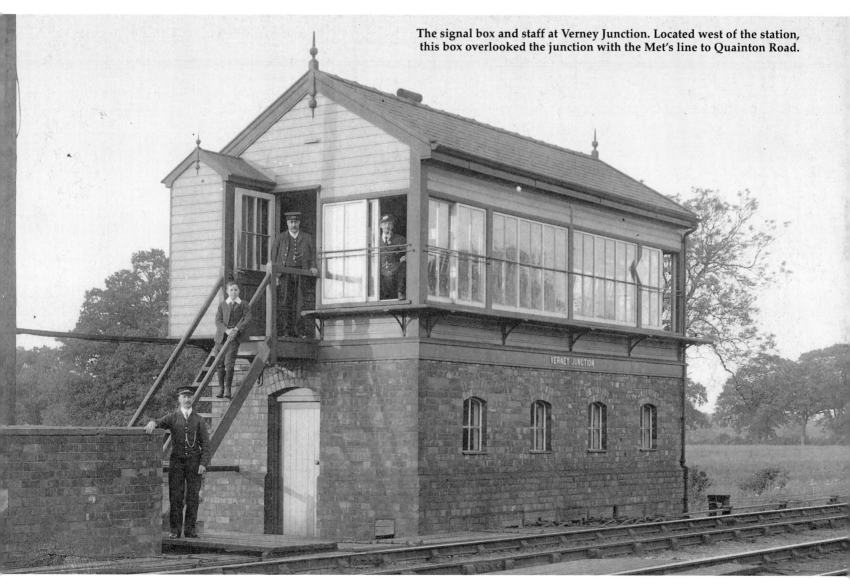

The signal box and staff at Verney Junction. Located west of the station, this box overlooked the junction with the Met's line to Quainton Road.

VERNEY JUNCTION

Locomotive No. 8367 at Verney Junction with the 5.27 p.m. service from Bletchley to Banbury, 2 May 1936. Verney Junction was added to the branch on 23 September 1868 for the opening of the branch to Aylesbury.

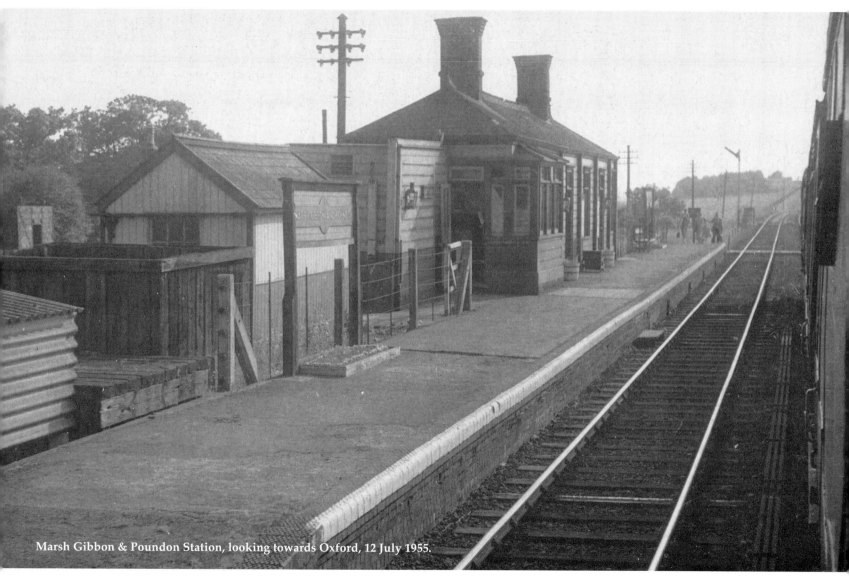

Marsh Gibbon & Poundon Station, looking towards Oxford, 12 July 1955.

Marsh Gibbon & Poundon, 16 June 1958. This station was a later addition to the line, opening on 2 August 1880.

Quainton Road line (Aylesbury to Quainton Road)

Passenger service withdrawn	3 September 1966	*Stations closed*	*Date*
Distance	6.4 miles	Waddesdon Manor *	30 November 1935
Company	Metropolitan & Great Central Joint Committee	Quainton Road	4 March 1963

Great Central Railway No. 260, a fast Atlantic 4-4-2, at Waddesdon Manor heading an express to Marylebone.

* Renamed Waddesdon on 1 October 1922.

Locomotive No. 5594 at Quainton Road with the 3.30 p.m. service from Verney Junction to Aylesbury, 15 March 1930.

QUAINTON ROAD

This line was originally the southern half of the Aylesbury & Buckingham Railway. Running from the county town to the London & North Western's Oxford Branch at Verney Junction, the Aylesbury & Buckingham was opened on 23 September 1868. Initially, the scheme was backed by the London & North Western and envisaged a connection to that company's Aylesbury Branch. But the London & North Western became wary of valueless branches and refused to have anything to do with the idea (at this time it also repudiated the company which built what was to become the Midland's Hemel Hempstead Branch). However, the Great Western stepped in to work the line via an end-on junction to its Aylesbury Branch. For the next thirty years the Aylesbury & Buckingham was a little used country backwater, its single track trailing languidly through the Buckinghamshire flatlands. But this was to change. The Met, heading north, snapped up the impecunious local line for use as a convenient link to its southward-moving sometime-friend, the Manchester, Sheffield & Lincolnshire (Great Central from 1897). Merging the Aylesbury & Buckingham in 1894, the Met rebuilt the line for fast through traffic. To cure a little tiff with the Great Central, the old Aylesbury & Buckingham was made property of a joint committee in 1906.

Quainton Road Station. The main line platforms are to the left, while the Brill Branch is on the right.

Under the joint committee's regime the line saw frequent fast Great Central expresses to the Midlands and Yorkshire, with local services mostly provided by the Met. However, there was little originating traffic from the surrounding small villages. This was the deciding factor for the cessation of Metropolitan line services north of Aylesbury in the mid-1930s. Services from Marylebone continued to use the line until the closure of the old Great Central main line. Since 1971 occasional specials have been run on the line in connection with the preservation group based at Quainton Road. In addition through freight trains also use the line on a limited basis.

Staines Branch (West Drayton to Staines West) *

Passenger service withdrawn	29 March 1985	*Stations closed*	*Date*
Distance	6 miles	Colnbrook Estate Halt	29 March 1965
Company	Great Western		

The Staines & West Drayton Railway was incorporated in 1873. However, due to financial and construction difficulties it wasn't until 9 August 1884 that the line could be opened as far as Colnbrook (including the two miles or so in Buckinghamshire), with completion through to Staines the following year. The local company was merged into the Great Western, which had always provided services, in 1900. The Staines Branch was fairly well used by passengers, especially from Colnbrook, and survived into the diesel era before closure. The line was also important for its goods traffic, especially the trading estates served along the route; the section from West Drayton to Colnbrook remains in use to various customers, including a fuel depot serving Heathrow Airport.

* Closed stations on this line that were in Middlesex were Colnbrook, Poyle Halt, Poyle Estate Halt, Yeoveney Halt and Staines West.

Thame line (Princes Risborough to Oxford) *

Passenger service withdrawn	7 January 1963	*Stations closed*	*Date*
Distance	16.6 miles	Bledlow	7 January 1963
Company	Great Western	Towersey Halt	7 January 1963

Bledlow Station, looking towards Oxford, 23 July 1955.

This line was built as an extension of the Wycombe Railway (see Wycombe line), initially to the small market town of Thame and later beyond to Oxford. The moving spirits were the elite of Thame, who vainly hoped that the railway would bring prosperity in its wake. The line between High Wycombe and Thame opened on 1 August 1862, with through running to Oxford starting two years later. After the opening of the Great Western & Great Central Joint line, the line operated mostly as a rural branch line serving Thame and several other small Oxfordshire towns and villages. It also formed an alternative route to Oxford from London (shorter than that presently used), but the Morris Cowley motorworks at the Oxford end was probably most important in terms of goods and passenger traffic in modern times. The five miles or so in Buckinghamshire were unimportant as Bledlow was a typical middle-of-nowhere country station, yielding only agricultural produce on the goods side, and Towersey was an unstaffed halt without goods facilities. The rails remain in place as far as Thame and until recently served an oil terminal there. The remains are slated for preservation.

* Closed stations on this line that were in Oxfordshire were Thame, Tiddington, Wheatley, Horspath Halt, Garsington Bridge Halt, Morris Cowley and Littlemore.

Towersey Halt, 16 June 1957. Opened on 5 June 1933, this was a typical Great Western structure of wood and corrugated iron.

Uxbridge High Street Branch (Denham Junctions to Uxbridge High Street) *

Passenger service withdrawn	1 September 1939	*Distance*	2 miles
		Company	Great Western

This very minor line to the old Middlesex market-town-turned-suburb was built as a branch of the Great Western & Great Central Joint line, although it was always owned and operated by the Great Western. The branch opened on 1 May 1907 and closed for goods in 1964. A very small part of the line (less than half a mile) was in Buckinghamshire.

* The closed station on this line that was in Middlesex was Uxbridge High Street.

Verney Junction line (Quainton Road to Verney Junction)

Passenger service withdrawn	6 July 1936	*Stations closed*	*Date*
Distance	5.9 miles	Granborough Road	6 July 1936
Company	Metropolitan & Great Central Joint Committee	Winslow Road	6 July 1936

Granborough Road, 1933. This was known as Grandborough Road until 1920.

LNER No. 8307 (an ex-GER 0-6-0 tank) at Winslow Road with the 6.20 p.m. service from Aylesbury to Verney Junction (coach No. 51905), 2 March 1936.

This was the northern half of the old Aylesbury & Buckingham Railway (for the Aylesbury to Quainton Road route see Metropolitan & Great Central). The Aylesbury & Buckingham was opened on 23 September 1868 to connect Aylesbury with the London & North Western's Oxford line, with connections from there to Buckingham – hence the company's title. The line passed to the Met in 1894 and to the Joint Committee in 1906. Just before the turn of the century this section was doubled and reconstructed. Rather more steeply graded than the southern half, but still substantially built with relatively frequent services including a through Pullman to Baker Street, it was nevertheless essentially a rural branch of the Met. Passenger services ceased not long after the takeover of the Met by London Transport in 1933. Goods traffic, mainly interchange, initially remained important but a goods-only link at Claydon between the Oxford line and the old Great Central was installed in 1940, effectively superseding this half of the old Aylesbury & Buckingham, which was completely closed in 1947. The route can be traced, but the trackbed has been partly absorbed back into the surrounding farmland.

Watlington Branch (Princes Risborough to Watlington) *

Passenger service withdrawn	1 July 1957	*Stations closed*	*Date*
Distance	8.8 miles	Bledlow Bridge Halt	1 July 1957
Company	Great Western		

Bledlow Bridge Halt, 23 July 1955.

This lightly built rural branch line, about two miles of which lay in Buckinghamshire, was constructed by the Watlington & Princes Risborough Railway and opened on 15 August 1872. The local company was absorbed by the Great Western in 1883. Passenger traffic was always light and the branch was an early casualty in British Railways' 'war' against the railway network. Goods traffic, however, was relatively substantial and until recently the line continued in use as far as Chinnor to serve a cement works. Bledlow Bridge possessed no goods facilities and was opened in 1906 in association with the introduction of steam railcar operation on the line. Despite the suffix the halt was nearer to the village than Bledlow Station on the Thame line.

* Closed stations on this line that were in Oxfordshire were Wainhill Crossing Halt, Chinnor, Kingston Crossing Halt, Aston Rowant, Lewknor Bridge Halt and Watlington.

Wotton Underwood line (Ashendon Junction to Grendon Underwood Junction)

Passenger service withdrawn	3 September 1966	*Stations closed*	*Date*
Distance	5.6 miles	Wotton	7 December 1953
Company	Great Central	Akeman Street	7 July 1930

The building of Wotton Station, 1906. The building still under construction on the left is the signal box.

Akeman Street Station, looking towards Calvert, 1932.

This line was built as an integral part of the Great Western and Great Central Joint scheme (see Introduction) and was essentially the section connecting the Great Western & Great Central proper with the Great Central's old main line. It is no exaggeration to say that the line went from nowhere to nowhere through the middle of nowhere! Its stations were early victims of economising, although the line was not built with local traffic in mind. This was a well-constructed route, straight as possible with slight grades, designed for fast through running. However, long distance travel shunned the line. Shortly after the line was opened on 2 April 1906, the Great Central and the Met came to terms. The quarrel between these two companies was one of the main reasons the Great Central became involved in the Great Western & Great Central in the first place. Consequently, the Great Western & Great Central was a second string so far as the Great Central was concerned – useful during rush hours when the Harrow to Quainton Road line was congested, but definitely secondary. After 1958 the line was little used and its solitary passenger train per week ceased when the Great Central main line was shut down. The line survived intact for a short while in connection with locomotive trials, but by the end of the decade the track south of Akeman Street had been removed. Until recently, the northern half of the line remained as a siding to a fertiliser plant.

Wycombe line (High Wycombe to Bourne End only)

Passenger service withdrawn	2 May 1970	*Stations closed*	*Date*
Distance	5.2 miles	Wooburn Green	2 May 1970
Company	Great Western	Loudwater	2 May 1970

Loudwater Station, *c.*1907.

The Wycombe Railway was opened between Maidenhead and High Wycombe on 1 August 1854. Although organised by local interests, which wished to connect the thriving south Buckinghamshire town to the main line, the Wycombe Railway was always in the pocket of the Great Western, who leased it at the time of opening and absorbed it in 1867. The line was built as broad gauge (7 ft 0¼ in.) but converted to standard in 1870. The section which was fated to be closed ran through pretty, wooded country. Loudwater and Wooburn Green served small villages which eventually became rather exclusive suburbs. The Maidenhead to High Wycombe section was effectively sidelined as a result of the completion of the Great Western & Great Central Joint line project in 1910, which put High Wycombe on a main line. Thereafter, the service pattern was somewhat mixed with through trains to Paddington, as well as local services to Oxford and Aylesbury. The Bourne End to Maidenhead line was to remain fairly prosperous, connecting as it did with the busy Marlow Branch (opened 1873). But the section on to High Wycombe dwindled. The intermediate stations were reduced to halt status in 1966 and the following year a limited service from Maidenhead to Wycombe was introduced. In 1970 even this ceased. The closed section was not busy on the goods side either. Near Wooburn Green was a siding to a paperworks, but neither station generated much else and the line ceased to be used by goods trains even before passenger closure. Certain sections of the old route have been used for new housing and so forth, but the greater portion of the alignment can still be traced.

Closed passenger stations on lines still open to passengers

Aylesbury Branch (Princes Risborough to Aylesbury)

Stations closed	*Date*
South Aylesbury Halt	5 June 1967

South Aylesbury Halt, looking towards Aylesbury town, 8 August 1959. This halt opened on 13 February 1935.

Great Western & Great Central Joint line

Stations closed	Date	Stations closed	Date
Penn Halt	31 October 1932	Ilmer Halt	7 January 1963
West Wycombe	3 November 1958	Haddenham **	7 January 1963
Princes Risborough *	2 April 1906		

West Wycombe Station. This photograph shows the original buildings of 1862 with evidence of the early phases of rebuilding for the coming of the Joint line. West Wycombe Church is in the background.

* Station resited – replacement currently in use.

** Haddenham & Thame Parkway, opened on 5 October 1987, is very close by.

Contractor's locomotive 'Norman', built by Hunslett in 1868, at Haddenham Station, *c.*1909. Note the 'steam navvies' in the background.

Haddenham Station, looking towards Princes Risborough, 15 April 1956.

Great Western Railway: Birmingham line

Stations closed	Date	Stations closed	Date
Dorton Halt	7 January 1963	Brill & Ludgershall	7 January 1963

A passenger train about to enter the platform loop at Brill & Ludgershall Station, c.1911. Little remains of the site today.

Great Western Railway: main line

Stations closed	Date	
Slough *	8 September 1864	* Station resited – replacement currently in use

Great Western Railway: Windsor Branch

Stations closed	Date
Chalvey Halt	6 July 1930